The Really Wild Life of Birds of Prey™

PEREGRINE FALCONS

DOUG WECHSLER

The Rosen Publishing Group's
PowerKids Press™

For Dori, with love.

Thanks to Kathy Clark of the New Jersey Division of Fish, Game & Wildlife and Dan Brauning of the Pennsylvania Game Commission for their help.

About the Author
Wildlife biologist, ornithologist, and photographer Doug Wechsler has studied birds, snakes, frogs, and other wildlife around the world. Doug Wechsler works at The Academy of Natural Sciences of Philadelphia, a natural history museum. As part of his job, he travels to rain forests and remote parts of the world to take pictures of birds. He has taken part in expeditions to Ecuador, the Philippines, Borneo, Cuba, Cameroon, and many other countries.

Published in 2001 by The Rosen Publishing Group, Inc.
29 East 21st Street, New York, NY 10010

First Edition

Book Design: Michael de Guzman

Photo Credits: pp. 4, 7, 12, 13, 15, 19, 20, 22 © Doug Wechsler/VIREO; p. 8 © F. K. Schleicher/VIREO; p. 11 © P. McLain/VIREO; p. 16 © J. Ruos/VIREO. All photographs from VIREO (Visual Resources for Ornithology), The Academy of Natural Sciences' worldwide collection of bird photographs.

Wechsler, Doug.
        Peregrine falcons/ by Doug Wechsler.
        p. cm. — (The really wild life of birds of prey)
    Summary: Describes the physical traits and behavioral habits of this bird of prey.
        ISBN 0-8239-5598-2 (lb : alk. paper)
        1. Peregrine falcon—Juvenile literature. [1. Peregrine falcon. 2. Falcons.] I. Title.
QL696.F34 W43 2000
598.9'6—dc21   99-059349

Manufactured in the United States of America

CONTENTS

THEY COME OUT OF NOWHERE

A noisy **flock** of **sandpipers** suddenly flies from the beach. As it lifts off, the flock squeezes together almost into a ball. This is a sure sign that a **predator** is in the air. Your eyes glance at the sky. From out of nowhere, a large, dark bird with pointy wings dives with its wings folded toward its body. As it reaches the flock of sandpipers, it opens its wings and pulls out of the dive. It hits a sandpiper with its sharp **talons** and grabs the bird in the air. Flapping swiftly, the dark bird flies into the distance and out of sight. You have just been introduced to the peregrine falcon, the great predator of the skies.

A peregrine falcon can dive at a speed of more than 150 miles (241 km) per hour.

LOOK! UP IN THE SKY!

If you look up at the sky almost anyplace in the world, you might see a peregrine falcon. About the only places peregrines are never found are the **poles**. Peregrines nest on six continents. Peregrines living in the far north, such as in Alaska, Canada, and Russia, **migrate** south in the fall. They are strong fliers. They cross deserts, mountains, oceans, and forests. The whole journey may be as much as 6,000 miles (9,656 km) each way.

Peregrines can be found almost anywhere except the North and South Poles. The word "peregrine" means wanderer.

DOUG SAYS

PEREGRINES CAN
FEED ON SMALL
BIRDS WHILE
MIGRATING.

DOUG SAYS

PEREGRINES HAVE A WINGSPAN OF 37 TO 46 IN. (94 TO 117 CM).

FASTEST BIRD IN THE WORLD

The pointy wings of the peregrine falcon are made for speed. When a peregrine flaps hard, it can fly at 60 miles (96.6 km) per hour going straight. When it dives after **prey**, a peregrine folds its wings and zooms down at an angle. It may reach speeds of more than 150 miles (241 km) per hour. This speed makes it the fastest bird on earth. No one has been able to measure its fastest speeds exactly.

A peregrine falcon's high-speed chases and dives make it able to catch everything from a sparrow to a duck.

PIGEON, BREAKFAST OF CHAMPIONS

Peregrine falcons eat other birds. They catch them with amazing dives and chases. Mostly they eat birds between the sizes of a sparrow and a small duck. Pigeons are fast-flying birds, but peregrines are champion fliers. In cities pigeons are often the breakfast of these champions. Peregrines like to eat pigeons. Once in a while, a peregrine will kill a bird as large as a goose. After the peregrine hits the bird with its talons, the peregrine lets the bird fall to the ground and eats it there.

In one day an adult peregrine falcon eats an amount of food equal in weight to two blackbirds. ▶

DOUG SAYS

PEREGRINES GET MOST OF THEIR WATER FROM PREY.

DOUG SAYS

MOST PEREGRINES ARE LIKELY TO NEST IN PLACES SIMILAR TO THE ONES WHERE THEY WERE BORN. IF A PEREGRINE GREW UP ON A LEDGE OF A BUILDING, IT IS LIKELY TO CHOOSE A BUILDING FOR ITS NEST SITE.

A SIMPLE NEST

Peregrine falcons do not waste their time building nests. Instead they find a ledge or hole in a cliff. They scrape a bowl shape out of the dirt on the ledge and lay their eggs there. Ever since people started building skyscrapers and huge bridges, peregrines have been nesting on them, too. Cliffs and buildings are safe places for peregrines to avoid most predators and to keep away from people. They have a great view from the opening of the nest site. They can see their enemies from far away and watch birds flying below them.

The female peregrine lays about three to five eggs each spring. Many choose sites like this one inside a bridge beam.

HUNTING SCHOOL

Peregrine falcon parents help to teach their young the skills needed to hunt. One trick the parents use is to drop prey off of a ledge. This forces the young bird to go into a dive. The young falcon tries to catch the prey in the air before the prey hits the ground. The young soon learn to take birds from the parents' talons in flight, high above the ground. A young falcon will roll over beneath the parent and grab the bird while flying upside down. Young peregrines often hunt insects in the air and eat them in flight. This is good practice before they learn to chase speedy birds.

When the baby peregrines hatch, they are covered with soft, fluffy white feathers, called down. Adults have a blue-gray back, wings, and tail. The underparts of peregrines are a white or light tan color.

THE DANGER OF DDT

DDT is a powerful chemical that kills insects. Unfortunately, it kills more than just insects. DDT was sprayed in many parts of the United States and other countries during the 1950s and 1960s to kill insects. Birds ate the insects that were sprayed. The DDT ended up in the birds' bodies. Peregrine falcons ate the birds and stored DDT in their bodies. Female peregrines with DDT in their bodies laid eggs with thin shells or eggs that would not hatch. By 1965, almost all of the peregrine falcons in the eastern United States had died. Scientists learned from the birds how dangerous DDT is. The chemical was **banned** in the United States in 1972.

Scientists discovered that the chemical DDT greatly harmed peregrines, especially the shells of their eggs.

BIRD SCIENTISTS TO THE RESCUE

Dr. Thomas Cade was an **ornithologist**. An ornithologist is a scientist who studies birds. Dr. Cade had a plan to rebuild the peregrine population. To do this, his team would breed, or raise, lots of young peregrines in **captivity**. Then the peregrines would be **hacked** into the wild. Hacking is a way to release birds into the wild slowly while they learn to hunt. The birds are placed in a tower with a box on top that has a doorway. Food is brought to them so they always have plenty to eat. As they learn to fly, they return for their meals. Soon they start to hunt, but dinner is always waiting until they can catch enough birds to feed themselves.

Ornithologists put boxes out to help peregrines nest on bridges and buildings.

THE GREAT COMEBACK

Other ornithologists and many volunteers helped Dr. Thomas Cade with the peregrine falcons. Six thousand young peregrines were released into the wild in less than 20 years. With the chemical DDT banned, the birds had a chance to live. In 1975, ornithologists counted only 159 peregrine nests in North America. By 1997, there were 1,650. The program to save the peregrines in America was a success. In 1999, the peregrine falcon was taken off the **endangered species list**.

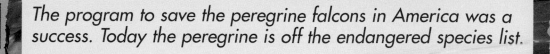

The program to save the peregrine falcons in America was a success. Today the peregrine is off the endangered species list.

BIRD OF KINGS

Peregrine falcons are great hunters. People train them and use them for hunting. When people use falcons to hunt, it is called **falconry**. After training the peregrine falcon for a long time, the falconer is ready to let the bird hunt. The falconer takes the peregrine to a good hunting area and lets it go. It flies high, then dives to catch a bird. The falconer whistles for the peregrine to return with the prey in its talons.

Falconry was popular in China more than 2,500 years ago. It has been called the sport of kings because it was popular among **noblemen** in Asia and Europe. The magnificent flight of the peregrine falcon still inspires many falconers and bird watchers today.

GLOSSARY

banned (BAND) Something that is not allowed.

captivity (kap-TIH-vih-tee) When an animal lives in a zoo or an aquarium instead of the wild.

DDT (D D T) A kind of insecticide, or poison meant to kill insects.

endangered species list (en-DAYN-jerd SPEE-sheez LIST) The names of species, or kinds of animals, that will probably die out if we do not protect them or the places where they live.

falconry (FAL-kun-ree) Keeping and training a bird of prey to hunt other animals for the keeper or falconer.

flock (FLOK) A group of the same kind of birds or animals keeping, feeding, or herding together.

hacked (HACKD) Having released birds slowly into the wild.

migrate (MY-grayt) When large groups of birds, animals, or people move from one place to another.

noblemen (NOH-bul-men) Members of royalty or other high-ranking people in a kingdom.

ornithologist (or-nih-THAH-luh-jist) A scientist who studies birds.

poles (POHLZ) The northern and southern ends of the earth. The Arctic is the northern end and the Antarctic is the southern end.

predator (PREH-duh-ter) An animal that kills other animals for food.

prey (PRAY) An animal that is eaten by another animal for food.

sandpipers (SAND-pye-purz) Small birds that live in wetlands and have long beaks.

talons (TA-luns) Sharp, curved claws on a bird of prey.

INDEX

WEB SITES

To learn more about peregrine falcons, check out these Web sites:

http://www.raptor.cvm.umn.edu/
http://www.acnatsci.org/vireo (Readers can order a raptor slide set.)